LET'S-READ-AND-FIND-OUT SCIENCE®

STAGE 1

DINOSAURS BIG and Small

by Kathleen Weidner Zoehfeld • illustrated by Lucia Washburn

HarperCollins*Publishers*

For Gwendolyn Rose
—K. W. Z.

For Jennifer
—L. W.

Special thanks to Jenny Lando
of the American Museum of
Natural History for her time
and expert review

The *Let's-Read-and-Find-Out Science* book series was originated by Dr. Franklyn M. Branley, Astronomer Emeritus and former Chairman of the American Museum–Hayden Planetarium, and was formerly co-edited by him and Dr. Roma Gans, Professor Emeritus of Childhood Education, Teachers College, Columbia University. Text and illustrations for each of the books in the series are checked for accuracy by an expert in the relevant field. For more information about Let's-Read-and-Find-Out Science books, write to HarperCollins Children's Books, 1350 Avenue of the Americas, New York, NY 10019, or visit our website at www.letsreadandfindout.com.

HarperCollins®, ☙®, and Let's Read-and-Find-Out Science®
are trademarks of HarperCollins Publishers Inc.

DINOSAURS BIG AND SMALL
Text copyright © 2002 by Kathleen Weidner Zoehfeld
Illustrations copyright © 2002 by Lucia Washburn
Printed in the U.S.A. All rights reserved.
www.harperchildrens.com

Library of Congress Cataloging-in-Publication Data
Zoehfeld, Kathleen Weidner.
  Dinosaurs big and small / by Kathleen Weidner Zoehfeld ; illustrated by Lucia Washburn.
    p.   cm. — (Let's-read-and-find-out science. Stage 1)
  ISBN 0-06-027935-4. — ISBN 0-06-027936-2 (lib. bdg.) — ISBN 0-06-445182-8 (pbk.)
    1. Dinosaurs—Size—Juvenile literature.   [1. Dinosaurs—Size.]   I. Washburn, Lucia, ill.   II. Title.
III. Series.
QE861.5.Z64   2002
567.9—dc21
                                                                                    00-059695
                                                                                    CIP
                                                                                    AC

Typography by Elynn Cohen   1 2 3 4 5 6 7 8 9 10 ❖   First Edition

DINOSAURS
BIG
and
Small

Everyone knows, some dinosaurs were BIG!

How big?

One of the biggest of all dinosaurs was the huge beast called *Diplodocus*.

6

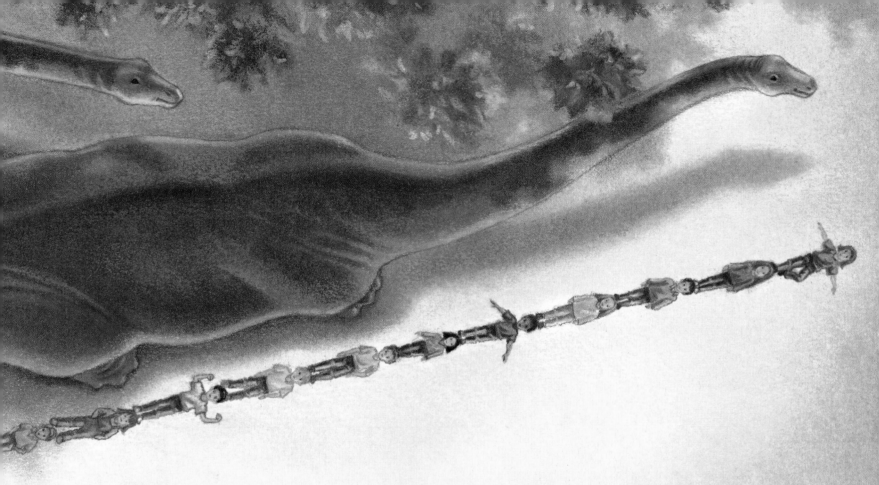

You are probably about 4 feet tall, more or less.

From the tip of its snout to the end of its tail, a *Diplodocus* was 89 feet long. That's longer than 22 kids laid out, head to foot.

A kid weighs about 75 pounds. *Diplodocus* weighed about 24,000 pounds—as much as 320 kids together!

The blue whales that swim in the oceans
today are the largest animals ever.
But the largest animals that have ever lived on land were
a group of dinosaurs called the sauropods. *Diplodocus* is one
type of sauropod.

All sauropods were plant eaters. They had small heads, long necks and tails, and four strong legs.

9

How do we know how big a sauropod was?

If we have enough bones from a dinosaur's skeleton, it is not hard to measure how long the animal was. But figuring out how much a dinosaur weighed is not so easy.

You can weigh yourself on a scale. No one can put a sauropod on a scale. And even if we could, we have only the fossil bones to go on. We cannot know exactly how heavy a dinosaur was. Scientists can only study the skeleton and make a good guess about how much fat and muscle the living animal might have had.

12

One of the longest sauropods ever found is the gigantic *Seismosaurus*. It was more than 130 feet long. A school bus is about 30 feet long. *Seismosaurus* was longer than 4 school buses parked end to end.

Brachiosaurus was a sauropod with thick, sturdy bones. It was one of the heaviest dinosaurs.

Brachiosaurus's front legs were longer than its hind legs. It held its neck and head high. It could nibble on leaves at the tops of the tallest trees.

Brachiosaurus may have weighed as much as 160,000 pounds.

A grown-up elephant weighs about 10,000 pounds.

One *Brachiosaurus* would weigh as much as 16 elephants.

Scientists say *Brachiosaurus* weighed 16 elephant units.

15

Argentinosaurus weighed even more than the hefty *Brachiosaurus*. It may have weighed as much as 200,000 pounds, or 20 elephant units.

A few bones have been found from other sauropods that were even bigger.

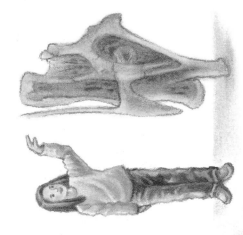

One vertebra, or backbone, from a *Sauroposeidon* is five feet tall.

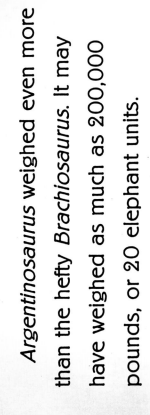

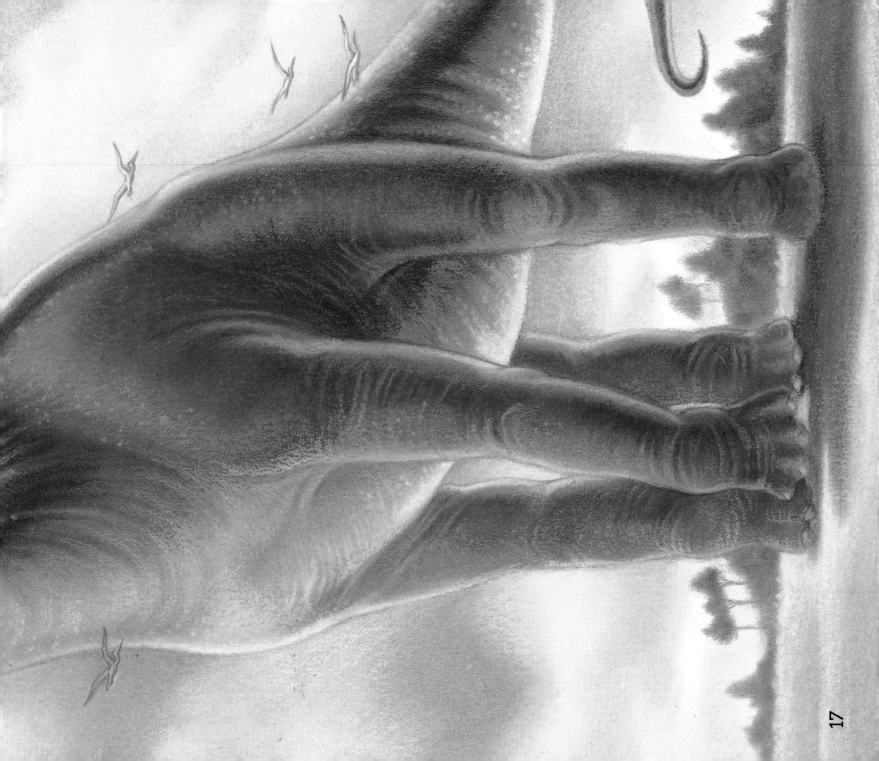

18

The biggest meat-eating dinosaurs, such as *Giganotosaurus*, hunted sauropods for supper. *Giganotosaurus* weighed less than 2 elephant units—small compared to the huge plant eaters. But *Giganotosaurus* had a mouth full of sharp teeth the size of bananas. And the big meat eaters may have hunted in groups.

actual size

Not all dinosaurs were gigantic, though.
Some, like *Iguanodon*, were medium-sized.
Iguanodon weighed about as much as
133 kids, or almost one elephant.

Iguanodon gathered in herds and grazed on ferns, much the same as today's elephant herds graze on bushes and grass.

21

Some dinosaurs were even smaller than *Iguanodon*.
How much smaller?
The sharp-clawed meat eater *Deinonychus* was much smaller.
It was only about the size of a grown man.
Some dinosaurs weren't any bigger than you.
Coelophysis was another meat eater. It was about as heavy as one kid. You wouldn't have wanted to tangle with a *Coelophysis*, though. They were so fierce, they sometimes ate their own babies!

The feathered dinosaur, *Caudipteryx*, was turkey-sized. *Compsognathus* was even smaller. You could have carried it in your arms like a cat! *Compsognathus* ran fast on its birdlike legs. It caught and ate insects and small lizards with its sharp claws and teeth.

Most scientists say that small meat-eating dinosaurs like *Caudipteryx* and *Compsognathus* may have been the ancestors of today's birds.

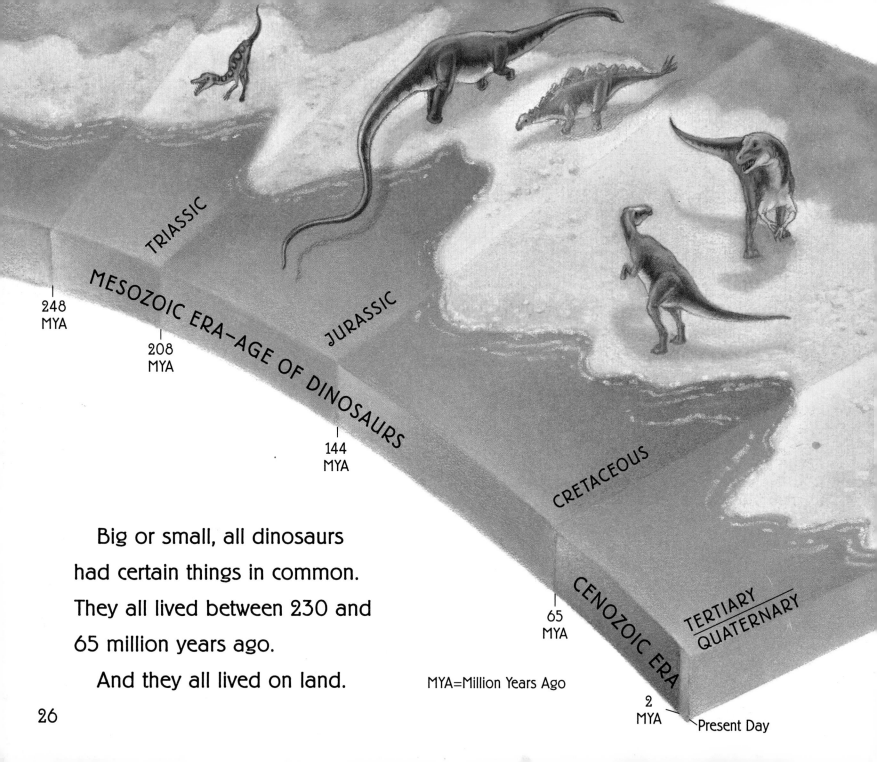

TRIASSIC

248 MYA

MESOZOIC ERA–AGE OF DINOSAURS

208 MYA

JURASSIC

144 MYA

CRETACEOUS

65 MYA

CENOZOIC ERA

TERTIARY

QUATERNARY

Big or small, all dinosaurs had certain things in common. They all lived between 230 and 65 million years ago.

And they all lived on land.

26

MYA=Million Years Ago

2 MYA

Present Day

All dinosaurs walked tall, with their legs directly beneath them. They did not sprawl on bent legs like lizards or crocodiles. And they all laid eggs like today's birds and reptiles.

dinosaur eggs from
unknown species

oviraptor
egg

maiasaur
egg

chicken
egg

One of the tiniest dinosaur skeletons ever found belonged to a *Mussaurus*. This *Mussaurus* died as a baby and was fossilized. It was so small, you could have cradled it in your hands like a little bird.

All baby dinosaurs were small—like all babies that hatch from eggs.

Some types of dinosaurs hatched from their eggs and grew up to be BIG. Other types grew up but stayed small.

From huge, lumbering *Diplodocus* to quick, little *Compsognathus*, dinosaurs came in many different shapes and sizes.

Find Out More About the Size of Dinosaurs

(1) *Argentinosaurus* (ar-gen-TEEN-oh-soar-us)
length: 115 to 130 feet; weight: 80 to 100 tons*

(2) *Brachiosaurus* (brak-ee-oh-SOAR-us)
length: 67 to 85 feet; weight: 70 to 80 tons

(3) *Caudipteryx* (caw-DIP-ter-iks)
length: 3 feet; weight: 20 pounds

(4) *Coelophysis* (see-lo-FIE-sis)
length: 10 feet; weight: 40 to 75 pounds

32

(5) *Compsognathus* (komp-sug-NAY-thus)
length: 2 to 4 feet; weight: 6 to 7 pounds

(6) *Deinonychus* (die-NON-ni-kus)
length: 10 feet; weight: 130 pounds

(7) *Diplodocus* (di-PLOD-uh-kus)
length: 82 to 89 feet; weight: 11 to 12 tons

(8) *Giganotosaurus* (jig-ah-NO-tuh-SOAR-us)
length: 47 feet;
weight: 8 to 9 tons

(9) *Iguanodon* (ig-WHAN-oh-don)
length: 29 feet; weight: 4 to 5 tons

(10) *Mussaurus* (moo-SOAR-us)
length: (baby) 8 inches;
weight: less than 1 pound
(too small to be pictured here)

(11) *Seismosaurus*
(SIZE-moh-SOAR-us)
length: 110 to 170
feet;
weight: 30 to
50 tons

*One ton equals 2,000
pounds. An elephant
weighs about 5 tons.

33